Outside,
America

SARAH DE LEEUW

OUTSIDE, AMERICA

NIGHTWOOD EDITIONS

2019

Nightwood Editions
P.O. Box 1779, Gibsons, BC, VON 1VO, Canada
www.nightwoodeditions.com

EDITOR: Amber McMillan
COVER DESIGN & TYPOGRAPHY: Carleton Wilson

Nightwood Editions acknowledges the support of the Canada Council for the Arts,
which last year invested $153 million to bring the arts to Canadians throughout the country.
Nous remercions le Conseil des arts du Canada de son soutien. L'an dernier, le Conseil
a investi 153 millions de dollars pour mettre de l'art dans la vie des Canadiennes et des
Canadiens de tout le pays. We also gratefully acknowledge financial support from
the Government of Canada and from the Province of British Columbia through
the BC Arts Council and the Book Publishing Tax Credit.

This book has been produced on 100% post-consumer recycled, ancient-forest-free paper,
processed chlorine-free and printed with vegetable-based dyes.

Printed and bound in Canada.

LIBRARY AND ARCHIVES CANADA CATALOGUING IN PUBLICATION

De Leeuw, Sarah, author
Outside, America / Sarah de Leeuw.

Poems.
Issued in print and electronic formats.
ISBN 978-0-88971-354-3 (softcover).--ISBN 978-0-88971-143-3 (ebook)

I. Title.

PS8607.E2352O98 2019   C811'.6   C2018-904794-1
                                               C2018-904795-X

CONTENTS

Outside

America

OUTSIDE

ROGUE STARS

Think about Lite-Brite says the MIT post-doctoral scientist.
How even if we can't see it, there's still light behind
        the opaque, black paper.
Our galaxies are like the pegs punched through that paper.
Bright and easy to spot, taking up all the attention.
But there's still light.
Behind the opaque, black paper.
So much light we can't see, focusing just on the holes.
Which makes me think about glossy, thin-papered
        entertainment magazines.
The ones in the grocery store.
With the stars who take up my attention.
When I'm buying tuna or a plastic box of pre-washed spinach.
When I want to be thinking something profound. Something
        poetic.
About my father who passed away.
About the snow touching warm car hoods in the parking lot
        outside, disappearing.
About the hands of a man who carves stone in the Arctic,
        a documentary I saw.
But those galaxies are so easy to spot.
Being one of them. Obvious.
Oblivious to the light behind the black.

OCTOBER CHANTERELLING

Listen, my father says standing
downslope from the hiking trail trying

to teach me about details, about
being careful, so really he means *look,*

pointing out moss separating where a nurse
log lifts as it rots, shrinks, shifts skyward,

an opening for leaf buildup,
for mushrooms in semi-sandy close

to coastal soil covered with hemlock
needles, dead devil's club, the odd

softened, yellowed skunk cabbage
decaying beside tea-coloured, tannin

creeks flowing beachward, the sea
stretching to Japan from where

my father never tires of telling me,
those salt-roughened turquoise glass

balls float to us, how distance
is really small if you account for currents,

how no matter how long and strong
the lichen looks, it remains fragile,

how one should not rip out other
species in the hunt for chanterelles

and the long-gilled stems of edibles
should be cut, orangey-gold stubs

left in the ground for next year because
everything that grows on earth is left

by something else, even daughters
who will leave and cross oceans or those

two red cedars, twins attached
at ankle and neck, *when one falls the other*

will crumble; so my father is also saying
listen, I will die one day too: *look.*

FLYING NORTH, SNOW ON CLEAR-CUTS BELOW

I

lung x-rays   scans of every smoking
lumberjack   huge inhaling smears

of white   then grey overlay smudge
imaged lung on lung on lung

rib curve shadow   thicker snow
at the edges   of burn lines   touching trees

backlit   black.   where the doctor points
circling the patchy smudge

milkyness shot   with stump   clots
a creamy skid   of dull film layering

the scatterings scattered   patterns
logged   bronchial   hackings

II

as if whales   skyscraper sized   swam
in great circles   underground *exhale exhale!*

their foaming froth   bust
through   crust

as if herds of bison   gulping
for air   nostrils splayed   open

were suddenly fossils   laid bare
dust settling   on scratched slate

III

not the ocean   though similar
the way water reflects   a stormy

sky   the way   waves peak
split   disappear into   waterclouds

not the ocean   though similar
the way fallen forests   are flung

along shorelines   the way salt
settles like spit on lips

opened and opened
bending with no end

LAKELAND SAWMILL

Imagine us making love.

It's not actually the making
that's important here,
but the explosion.

People in small northern towns
might be making love at 9:44 p.m.
on a Monday night, mid-April,
snow still on the ground, an idling
logging truck pulled off some icy
highway, trains groaning
under lumber.

Concentrate on the *image*
of us making love. Yes, that's it.

When I come in after walking
the dogs, you notice my new toque,
light blue, smelling faintly of pulp.
You tuck my hair behind my ear,
take my hand.

We weren't making love,
but you see we could have been
if we hadn't decided to watch TV.

Maybe then, the ball of fire
would've added something, not just
shaken the couch, the undone dishes,

the windows, us, flipping channels
and wondering at all the sirens,
the slow scent of smoke.

Sawdust is the thing of it,
a bit more beige than snow,
easier to pull into your lungs,
to spontaneously ignite.

Someone might well have detonated
dynamite inside a live animal.

How to look each other in the eye
if we had made love
at those ragged edges?

Ribs blown to smithereens,
shattered scaffolding across
the loading dock, the innards of a kiln,
fresh pine two by fours wedged
vertically into the disaster-thawed,
muddy slop of a dry-land sort.

Step
Stone
Sand
Step
Pack
Stone
Seagulls
Step
Sea
Young whale
Stone
Stone
Boulder
Wolf
Sand
Mussel
Step
Sand
Sky
Sea
Step
Moss
Oyster
Plastic float
Salmon
Step
Step
Stone
Sand

Step
Stone
Sand
Seagull
Stone
Root
Step
Sea otter
Step
Dead whale
Sand
Step
Boulder
Lamb's quarters
Kelp
Step
Sea anemone
Stone
Sky
Sea
Sand
Alder
Step
Step
Stone
Heron
Clam
Step
Sand

Step
Step
Sand
Step
Bear
Salvaged fir log
Stone
Sea lion
Stone
Step
Sand
Step
Boulder
Sand
Kelp
Barnacle
Step
Driftwood
Sky
Sea
Stone
Step
Blackberry
Stone
Sand
Step
Step
Sand
Night

Stone
Sand
Stone
Step
Step
Step
Slippery kelp
Sea
Sand
Step
Stone
Boulder
Boulder
Net
Step
Step
Fireweed
Step
Sky
Sea
Step
Step
Step
Salal
Step
Creek
Stone
Tent
Kingfisher

OUR DIFFERENT LIFE

So much like before, almost boring,
the slow decay of window caulking,
the cold creep of winter air,

small arguments about personal
responsibility, climate change, energy
efficiency, our own heat waning,

falling into bed exhausted, negotiating
your ex-wife—who I understand
more and more—your children, texting

about the volcanic eruption in Japan—
the kind of thing about which we expect
forewarning, expect to be saved—

the news of hikers gulping in pebbles
and hot ash as I pull the blue-grey
exoskeleton from farmed, northern

striped shrimp, my fingers cold
under the tap's running stream, I wonder
when it changed from making love

before dinner to cooking alone,
expected now to nurse you in old age,
the role your wife once had, unwarned.

WHEN I MARRY FOX

September-October collision, colour
of sockeye salmon, spawning-spent
beneath floating leaf decay, denless.

The dishwasher, the La-Z-Boy, even
the lawn mower, broken and useless.
Husbandless, I stare full of envy
at the diamonds of other women.

Bear, beaver and even bull moose
have all said no. Like a hard-boiled egg
lodged in my throat: loneliness.

And did I mention the selkies?
Despite seal-fingered, flippery children,
their rot-salt stink of sea and tidal flats,
their men are shored. Beached.

Then Fox nip-knocks for me, leg lifted,
piss-sharp smell ripe as the ping bite
of high-bush cranberries.

I will wed you, wed you, wed you, he yips.
My hairless white body looming, his
promise of torn-up alley cats convincing
me: forgo silver stilettos, forget lace.

His bedroom is lined in downy owl fluff,
a neck he cracked years back. At first,
his teeth draw blood from my nipples,

razory little slices. He tugs at me like
he's tearing at tough, fresh roadkill.
Slowly calcification takes hold. My skin
thickens, his winter fur comes in full.

In our new year, when humans thumb
corks off bubbly-popping party sparklers
and snap open tin-foiled Christmas

crackers, he says: *It's time to sell my hide.*
Pelting time. This is what he offers
our world. Transforming briefly to man
then crawling back to me, bled.

He muzzle-shuffles gifts toward me,
exhausted. A restaurant packet of salt.
A bottle cap. A bright blue Steller's

jay feather. Of course I wait, now
I'm a fox-wedded wife. Our milky,
furless pups flipping inside me.
As if from drowning, springs life.

HOW TO CONVEY THAT DYING REALLY IS LONELY

It matters how, for instance, your daughters
do not visit, only calling once—maybe twice—

a month from far away, from a city with a river
you refuse to call a river, flanked with paved

sidewalks, not shores or banks, a gassy water
highway, nothing wild or untamed left, only

reintroduced salmon, opposite of those you
miss fishing in northern streams, a dog at

your side, now you watch him every morning
after you've taken a flight of pills knowing

he will outlive you, knowing the snow outside
may be the last snow you'll see, you can't see

the cells as they metastasize to pelvis just
like you can't see the jays, the chickadees or

the flickers, but you hear them like you dream
of cancer being white, an invisible racket

of noise you have to fall asleep with, knowing
it's all inside you. You wake up to the news

of an Olive Ridley sea turtle carried north
on ocean currents from Pacific coast Mexico,

life cooling away, found by crab fishermen
near Alaska, a slack-beaked face dappled jade

green, skin like light on a tropical sea,
how a woman named him Frank, wrapped

him in a blanket to warm him, how that didn't
work so she drove his body around town

in the hatchback of a rusting Honda Civic,
a sample specimen, a dead animal far from home.

EVERYDAY, ORDINARY, JUST-AFTER-WORK SONNET

When you're thinking twice about asking her to dance,
right 'round the living room and through the double-
glass doors, past that now not-so-new granite-topped
kitchen counter you both joked about making love
on, at least once, before dinner, then think again, think
again about your neighbour who hoped he'd heard
ornithology and thought about a rockery of herons
in cottonwood trees when instead the doctor said
oncology and his wife began to sob, some memory
of distraction, dandelions too high in the front lawn,
clipping the baby's fingernail too low, a cotton ball
pressed too tightly against a boil of blood that never
needed a Band-Aid. Make it a slow dance, close, the kind
without weeds, bright yellow, the opposite of putting off.

FORD'S RIGHT WHALE

We're not talking the Model-T here,
not stretching for some
metaphor
about a curvaceous beast, huge and sleek, alighting skyward,

breaking surface tension, busting
all expectations, breath-taking.

No illusion to the Fiesta, that right on,
fuel-efficient machine
so plentiful the company made a killing

and North American families
went wild again,
even Mustangs got a gunning-up

like the assembly line meant something, like
Detroit wasn't akin to a salt flat
where once there'd been an ocean.

Cars have nothing to do with this whale.

They're right because surely god must have designed them
especially for slaughter, so rightly proportioned.

Right amounts of blubber.
Right-sized baleen, perfect for corsets.
Right size to transport, they float with ease.
Right because they're docile.
Right because they stick close to shore.

It's just wild, how right they were.

Now they're like the Holy Grail say biologists, the Holy Grail
of whale.

Kind of funny

how we drive around on our superhighways
bumping into each other, so close we sometimes smell
the low tide, salt-rot of each other's sweat.

How there's no more
than a couple hundred right whales

left.

How on a Thursday in June, John Ford saw one,
a once-in-a-lifetime spotting and watched her
day and night, the first sighting of a right whale
in North Pacific waters since 1951.

I think he must
have fallen in love.

How they must lose
sight of each other for better
parts of a century.

Ford's right whale lolled, rolled
                              back exposed to the horizon,
                              black-barnacled skin stretched

over the space between them.

Maybe right whales
take ships for company now.

FLANK

Let go from the pulp mill
equals cold-throated
cheek pressed against
the containment wall
of a settling pond.

Tea-coloured chemical
soup, lockjaw underbite
means you feel gimped.
The men, the hard hats,
the sludge rattling skyward.

Something like weeping
except pointless,
a cut block, a cut bank,
a cut back, a tender
peeling back.

You see your own shadow
move on the snow's surface
like it's getting out from
under you too. There is rain,
rain on the rotting snow.

A mangled call, maybe
a bull moose at darkness's
rim, something just outside
the reach of orange
emergency lights.

Something like a heave,
breathing, alive, something
with tissue and tendons
beyond the parking lot.

CAUTION CURVE

We are every child, every horse, every once-
prefaced-with-caution animal all surging

across a bridge, over railway tracks, over
a river, first steel then blowing heat

under breaking-blue-sunrise light, ice
steaming on this calamity highway,

all our muscles knotted, white breath
and knuckles calling to winter, thickened

fur to cantering parents abandoned
in fields, in kitchens or forgotten bunk beds—

we're going too fast, too fast, our vehicles
in some near-past, we join where prop-planes

drop through garage roofs, through barn
rafters, through signs ignored, the turbulence

a fist: don't make the turn, don't make so tight
a turn, but   by then   the world has   bent.

DRONE NOTES ON CLIMATE CHANGE

Early in every summer, rare,
still-healthy, beluga-whale populations
migrate south. This year, drones shoot

video footage. More than fifty
thousand animals congregate where
scientists say *the whales simply*

like to meet. Where the Seal, Churchill
and Nelson Rivers empty into Hudson Bay's
western region, where sea ice is retreating.

Drone-shot from above, the belugas
are white punctuations on an old
elementary school blackboard. Squiggly

cursive curls, moving sentences swirl
a not-quite-new, yet wholly indiscernible
language, the whales meet. They

touch. Chalky, grammar-like clusterings
in love. What whaley words made of
whaleness! What wet, mammally sayings!

NIAGARA FALLS

It's true the world always drops off
at the horizon. But not quite like this.
Heaps of kidney-coloured soil

bulldozed against landfill dumps
and billboards advertising Hooters
and Vision Care, side by side,

plumes of mist rise on the other side
of casinos, wax-form, open-mouthed
Katy Perry like a hardened blow-up

doll, legs apart, we are asked to don
bright pink ponchos, the ferry slippery
with rush-churn river spray

camouflaging the shit-stained rocks
of nesting gulls screeching
in the showery air, all milk mist.

What a watery canyon, what a border:
country against country, with us
looking to where the world drops off.

WHAT WOMEN DO TO FISH

Well we eat them, raw of course,
sliced translucent, soft, orange.

Wishing our thighs chopstick thin,
leaving behind a silver slip of scale.

We flush exfoliating beads toward
them, nail-hard pearls with DDT
half-lives masquerading in lakes
as insect larva or seeds left after

we've turned over a new leaf,
scrubbed our wrinkles raw, refreshed
and stepping from the shower,
sun glinting on tiny orbs.

We offer protection from pregnancy,
knowing that, like us, a small part
of them is always afraid of rape,

or being left alone after a one-night
stand, our urine leaking out of us,
emptying estrogen and progestin
into distant watersheds.

KILLING DOGS

Twelve-year-olds'
summer morning.

Oars. Ocean.

Girls seated
in a salt-slicked
aluminum dinghy.

Fishing for salmon
(impossible), red
snapper, halibut,
Pacific cod.

Jigged bull-kelp
bullhead grinning.

Our lures,
our barnacle-sliced
lines, our limbs.

Then the noon
call to men
carried by water,
a bark, a bray,
strays

snapping unspayed,
scabby, feral,
rounded up in nets,
chucked
in fishing boats.

Dogs fed
to killer whales,
red-tide blood
foam, water squall

we wash off,
later as women,
our coast stained,
paddling just afloat.

SEVEN-F

is the most popular seat on an airplane,
nineteen-C the one everyone avoids.

I tend to choose fourteen-A, enjoying
the fuselage's middle, face pressed against

a cool, plastic window, people ahead
and behind me, lots of time to decide

between apple or tomato juice, which makes
me wonder if people wanting their preferred

seat tried early check-in for that German-
wings flight 9525. If they rolled or folded

their clothes trying to pack just one carry-on.
If they thought about pretzels, or had to be

asked twice to put their iPhones away, stop
texting. And this of course makes me feel

petty, without the depths of sympathy
others must feel, realizing every wrinkle

and annoyance—raising your voice
to your youngest child in the morning,

maybe not making love enough, eating
too many calories on Sunday without running

or forgetting your grandparent's birthday—
mean nothing. Because there is nothing

more profound and beautiful than simply
being alive, not having been killed on impact

with the Alps, breath stripped away,
oxygen masks dispensed, snow,

the unstoppable descent of a man
terrified about losing his sight.

HERSCHEL ISLAND

In my dream I am walking
on the edge of the world. No,

not some idea about the edge
of the world, but where half
the planet has sloughed away.

Calved. A jökulhlaup.

The quiet is very thick, almost
fatty. A warm tide of wind
streaming up from nothing.

Somewhere a noise, like whales
pinging each other, wails
and long sirening through water,
fathoms deep.

Mother whales, calving.
So it's not an apocalypse.
Not like Qikiqtaruk.
Flat layers of granite-greenstone
on permafrost. Endless ice
and the *flit flit flit flitting*,
no sound of Thule people.

Long ago melted.
In greasy streams of yellow oil.

Slushing off the last bowhead
whales of the Beaufort Sea.

Star-shaped splatters, constellations
of blood and blubber under
the feet of men dressed in wool
to their elbows, in slabs of skin,
flensing.

Baleen is a lacy comb.
Feathered bone.

The edge swallowing.

FAR-OFF NORTH

My friend Shyrl gets paid
to tell stories in hotel conference rooms—

beige walls, sweating water pitchers,
white tablecloths—about important,

morning work children were once
responsible for. Their fathers

would wake between pelts and ice,
say *Go look at the sky. Tell me each detail.*

Describing every cloud, filament of wind;
the weight of rain or snow or texture of air

was a child's job. Hunting and travelling
depended on those descriptions, *so imagine,*

laughs my friend Shyrl, *if a child
got it wrong.* Sometimes people wait days

for Shyrl's stories when Arviat weather
holds her in. Sometimes her husband

worries the polar bears are getting bolder,
or she asks about my mum, my dad's death.

Once I learned that her daughters
still name the husky pups, predicting future

temperaments, then sew prom
dresses from seal skin, silver-grey

speckled hide fashioned
in the style of *The Twilight Saga*.

HUNTING IN CITY DAYLIGHT

Blistering bright, so, sure it's a long
                         long shot

looking for a pregnant fox,
apple core in her mouth, sensing milk,
descending, we'll capture fiddleheads.

I lost the arrow, my aim's way off
                         off centre,

and yes, we do it best at night,
pit-lamping game, startled blind,
yellow-eyed creatures seeing nothing
at all. Still I love the way you take
aim, gunnysacking sparrows,
                         candy wrappers.

Our nets are stitched wide
                         wide open,

set with anchors festooned
from fallen chestnuts, my patent heels
sliding on long, plastic, kelp slips,
floating on the concrete sea,
we're gathering all that's soft-
                         shelled, hungry.

NEAR CN RAIL YARD, WINTER

1. A wasps' nest:

Where do the wasps go? Hinged
bodies slaughtered by the cold,
stripped of sounds, the hive
unravelled, papier-mâché,
skull-sized city hanging empty,
some seasonal derailment.

2. An eagle's nest:

Messy woven branches
smoothed by shit and feathers,
sliver of salmon skull, vertebrate
links a mother who lands home
whistling, white-head sunset
silhouetted, wings tucked against
wind, against slow snow

falling   on both.

BASE OF HUDSON BAY MOUNTAIN, SMITHERS

He visited me once.
Once.

I'm not even sure
if it happened. Or how.

A dream, perhaps,
he said it rained

last night.
Hard. All night.

The lakes, the rivers
are now

snow open
and water slaughter.

FOUND. BEHIND.

Baby pacifier. Plastic and latex. Blue mouth guard cracked. Nipple ripped. On sidewalk. Carney Street and Massey Drive. Early morning. Late summer.

Lottery ticket. Supersaver Extra number seven. Curled. Details of provincial gaming policy and regulations on back. Scratched silver face. 17th Avenue. 5:47 p.m. Early autumn.

Dog tag. Name: Spot. Bone shaped and copper. Green hue from exposure to elements. In a snow drift. Laurier Crescent. Afternoon. December.

Sock. Pink, purple, blue stripes. Size: child's. Frayed on top. Small hole in heel. In the ditch. McBride Crescent. Early morning. Early fall.

McDonald's milkshake cup. Size: medium. Wax coated. Flattened and indented with gravel. Early morning, well before sunrise. Patricia Avenue. Midsummer.

Underpants. Spiderman motif. Left leg ripped to waistband. On sidewalk near beer-bottle cap. Massey Drive. 6:16 a.m. July.

Beak of crow attached to portion of head. Eye. Dry and intact. Cream-coloured. On the edge of a well-trimmed lawn near a driveway. Mid-afternoon, after work. August seventeenth.

Cigarette filter. Players Extra Light. Stained with purple lipstick and surrounded by leaves. Mostly yellow from cottonwood. 15th Avenue. After 9:30 p.m. August.

Toque. Green. Hand-knit. Orange and yellow pompom. Stitched letters reading "Grandma's Love" in black. Frozen to concrete. Middle of road. Early evening. November.

Condom ring. Yellowed. Intact but detached from latex body. Stuck to gravel in parking lot. Running trails to university greenbelt and endowment lands. Noon. April.

Unidentifiable. Reminiscent of animal fat mixed with rust. On late winter snow. 5th Avenue. Very early morning. February.

House plant. Hoya. Mostly ripped apart and de-potted. Tightly bunched roots, white and light yellow. Some leaves intact. One bunch of waxy white flowers with dark pink centres. On sidewalk. 8th Avenue. Early morning. August.

Rear view mirror. Black and silver plastic. Single shard of glass still intact. Reflecting sky. Sidewalk of Demano Drive. 4:38 p.m. May twelfth.

Mars bar wrapper. "New dark chocolate." Opened perfectly on one end only. Resting on a yellow, cottonwood leaf. Loop four in Forests for the World Park. After work. Early October.

Body of a black bear cub. Compound fracture on left back leg, bone jutting through fur. Ear on pavement. Smear of blood, still glossy wet. No vehicle in sight. Shoulder of Highway 16. 6:48 p.m. September twenty-first.

Pepsi tin. Still perfectly intact. Unopened. Middle of highway, resting against dividing wall. 7:41 a.m. December twenty-third.

Bib. Cookie Monster on terrycloth side. Thin white plastic, shredded, on opposite side. Missing one green tie string. Stained with tomato sauce. After 10 p.m. Late summer.

Horse crop. Braided saddle-brown leather body. Black leather head, dangling by thin string. Moncton Crescent in College Heights. Evening. March.

Mattress. Queen-sized. Medium support. "Pillowey-soft technology." Sliced down the middle and resting against the flood-protection berm on Highway 37 north of Prince George. 9:35 a.m., Saturday during the Five Bridges Annual Road Race. September twenty-fourth.

Band-Aid. Fleshy pink with sand- and gravel-encrusted edges. Yellowed pus smear in centre of non-stick white centre. Under the Massey Drive overpass. Late evening. September.

Paperback novel with the cover torn off. Approximately 350 pages. Swollen and soaked with rain. Legible words include "terrorist," "spies" and "weapons of mass destruction." Oak Street 6:12 p.m. April.

YOU RE-ENTERED THE ATMOSPHERE

feeling weightless in the tin machine, pinned,
a few steps closer
to early-onset osteoporosis

                                      floating
into celebrity status
tweeting, YouTubing, and pleased
with your twilight twirling guitar
                             edge of blue-planet Earth
shining through your beyond-gravity rendition
                                of David Bowie's "Space Oddity."

Astronaut Commander Chris Hadfield calling
Major Tom, calling Major Tom, tell your wife
you love her very much.

The same day back
      down on the ground
      Captain Karl Lilgert is convicted
of criminal negligence causing death.

All us earthlings gather along
      northern coastlines, slack-jawed
      at the Pacific, Earth's great big,
      blue wondering

about that great white
               sinking ship,

allegations of stoned
sex on the *Queen of the North*'s bridge deck,
a former lover, still married,
the ship's second-in-command.

I imagine the two
                    who drowned.

Hearing the deep groans
                    of buckling metal
                    water-dulled thudding as cars
                    and transport trucks stack one
                    on   top   of   the   other
                    the draught hull
no longer vertical to the sea's surface, bowls
half-full of clam chowder
                    suddenly bumping against ceiling lights.

The ocean floor is like outer space, I hear.
Creaking portholes are your new songbirds.
                    The dawn is pitted, like beetle tracks
                    in driftwood
                    that sometimes sink close to you.

Slowly, sightless fish settle
in on starfish-patterned carpets.

You shut your eyes, learning
to dance standing on your
father's feet, moving
like a dream
across the living room floor,
everything suspended in water.

CENTRAL INTERIOR

It's summer in British Columbia
except not quite way up here,
even though the rivers are flooding
their banks, and the ground is loosening,
and my sister is living in Munich
right now, going to volleyball practices
in the evenings after work, working
out in purple spandex with her ropey
arms and platinum hair, a bombshell
who misses London, the city, the pace.

So when I'm driving early in the morning
to catch a flight going south, sky as light
as late last night, crusts of snow still
in the ditches, I catch my breath
at the small-townness of it all, at the hard-
drinking men hauling themselves into cabs
of logging trucks, mine and mill dust
floating in the air, a blur, inside

Dad are cells so sick it takes everything
to walk once around his garden
of new, sharp, tart rhubarb stems
sticking up almost like they hurt, so red
from composted earth, waxy leaves
opening, slackening fists.

UNRELATED INCIDENTS, OCTOBER AND NOVEMBER

We turn back the clocks; the first
mornings are full of light. *The Guardian*

posts an online video of an Omura's
whale swimming off the coast

of Madagascar. A woman in Vancouver
opens a can of Ocean Spray Cranberry

Sauce for Canadian Thanksgiving
and finds an entire garter snake coiled

inside, resting in a quiet, red death
nest. Omura's whales are so rare,

they have never before been filmed.
She said her surprise was so great,

she dropped the can opener,
end down, the silver metal tip

just missing her foot. November first,
2015 is the first time humans can watch,

again and again, the Omura's whale's
arrowed face open the sea. YouTube

is bursting and we are talking about
the last year, how, of the ten of us

having dinner together, two have lost
a baby, four have lost parents.

Not to mention pets and friends.
So many times, the surprise of animals.

Listen: nothing but the sound of water,
swimming. No one knows how few.

GROUND, BELOW

Even after the very worst
of things, the death of your son
or the news your only hope
rests in a double mastectomy,
removal of a subcutaneous
decay, you have to fly home.

These are the typhoon-touched
bodies in airports, filled
to the gills with grey-brown
debris-water, eyes bitten
by sand, guts full of bloated,
floating fish in the bellies

of mid-sized jets lifting off.
It's nearly impossible to squash
back sobs, all those little lakes,
muskeg bogs below, highways
leading to glaciers.

Something like flesh, a pattern.

It's so much easier
From   above.

WHEN YOUR MATE

She supposes the ashes,
>   wonders if geese are conscious, able,
>   making reasoned choices about going
>   south.

Two pines, unlikely amongst cottonwood, fireweed,
>   river ground exposed, low water, late
>   summer-salmon spawning, dried algae,
>   low sun.

Knows she will stay north, her husband
>   is the indent in sand under wind-fall
>   log and also moss, a shaggy mane.

Suddenly her hands. She recalls his hair, knee,
>   his whistling, a daughter, a daughter,
>   alder leaves green then gone, nothing
>   autumnal or gold.

Is that   a dog   so many crows,

>   some memory of pregnancy, ocean,
>   driftwood, sound is country-big, first
>   a star.

Perhaps a bear, cut-throat trout, a mourning cloak

>   butterfly, if she visits every day,
>   a chickadee calling winter, snow
>   of course, some vast new life.

The stain of remains, knuckle against sob, scattered.

AMERICA

EDGE OF PORT ANGELES

We passed that doe with the snapped leg standing,
panting, where suburban grass met cedar-chipped

garden of gnomes, mistaking her for a lawn ornament,
we passed and only blocks later registered

her quiver, so still a Sunday morning of sun, us two,
the sea on one side, waves sucking back and forth

against shore stones, we passed Oregon broadleaf
maples, ocean freighters in the distance, a hiking trail,

municipal recycling station, mountains with fresh snow,
sap sunk blood-red in willow trunks, us looking

for the grave of Raymond Carver who passed his entire
life here, buried in the Ocean View Cemetery, a short

hemlock walk from a small unpaved parking lot,
he died here where he'd lived all his fifty years,

small-town man under the weight of polished granite,
a Sunday morning, the sea on one side, love on the other.

OKLAHOMA I

The next day.

Head of a two-
and-a-half-
year-old boy.

Shaved.

Bald.

The razor's first
pass leaves
this path,
this wake
of grey, fragile
stubble.

Aerial view
of a crushed
corn field.

SURFACING BEHAVIOUR

Just shy of Alaska, catamaraning the contested
Dixon Entrance A-B Line somewhere south
of Prince of Wales Island, we're waiting

with whale-sized patience for the firm blue sea
to split open, our Canadian cellphones buzzing
with text links to American dialing codes

and roaming fee warnings, a cormorant, a distant
Tsimshian shell midden, where grass touches
tide, two Metlakatlas tilt totems and those

massive migrating mammals we want to see,
hoping some will be friendlies, breachers or bubble
netters, the stench of their baleen breath, fishy

and flint, their krilley shit strings of bright orange
recede, we are astounded silent, alive like a life
we never knew of, we're fools taking selfies,

trying to focus on us, bulky heads sky hopping,
nodding bristled faces, barnacled backs, an acrobat's
arc, a hump, our hearts hammering,

standing still, surrounded by ocean and pods,
small clouds on the horizon and sounds like zings,
strings on saw blades, they are so animal

but so me too, and so close I look exactly into
an eye and then down a blowhole, breathe in
her exhale and know nothing greater.

J-16, 8501

Mostly it's as if my father
is still alive because being
dead does not take away
his voice in my head or my
conversations with him
about J-16, the first female
born for decades in Puget
Sound's almost-dead orca
J-pod population. She's maybe
their last hope, teeth rakings
across her ovoid face marking
what scientists say was
an assisted birth, a killer-
whale midwife, wrenching
calf from uterus into ocean,
minutes before New Year's
Eve, so connecting her
with the two-day-old wreck
of Air Asia flight 8501,
cylindrical fuselage scarred,
chewed but full of the dead,
seatbelts buckled and black
box pinging like an orphaned
orca, the sea bottom a telegraph
line of currents, ever quieting
what sings and swims,
I hear my father answer.

OLD-GROWTH WILDFIRE

Outside Tucson, so not some namby-pamby,
moist, west coast thing, cedar or sequoia,

but cut, really ripped, rock-hard, bone-dry
saguaros popping open, flames ridin' dust

like in some Clint Eastwood flick, ponchos
flapping in the wind, the sound of stunt horses

galloping and carriages all dynamite-blasted up.
Dames hollering. No rain so no silver-bullet

quencher. I'm whistling that four-bar tune
and under an intestine-red sky, I ask the tavern

man to pour me a burning bourbon shot,
pelt that sucker back, smoke blind, dancing.

DRIVING THROUGH, RESERVATION

Go on, ride me bare
on a bow-backed mare

now we're down
in the Klickitat lows.

Dry oaks like smoking
truckers popping

their ears all along
those yellow highway

lines. Mount Adams
is burning anyhow,

yes sir, there's been
some fire here.

And in a place called
Status Pass, my hitch

came loose of trailer
loving when a cattle

guard got the best
of me. Had its way

like kettle corn
and spiced-up jerky

while somewhere
in a shady grove,

horses slept sideways,
casino losses calling

down the lightning
strikes, just this side

of me, then right
on through me.

OKLAHOMA II

The first time you hit
her, wallop her good,

                              you

          (pause) think about it.

It hasn't started to come

                              easy yet.

After a while, you don't even bother to look, bashing out,
                              simple as

what was the name of that twister?
touched down, bounced along
from Dallas to Wichita, peeling
the city skin right off Moore,

                          Oklahoma?

                          You forget.

Tornadoes don't get human names,
not Katrina, Ivan or Ike.

Slowly they blend into each other.

                   Ordinary events.

A dog trailing her leash, barking
outside a doorframe without a house.

Cicadas settled on the smooth,
sun-warmed, uncracked windshield
of a Toyota Landcruiser
dropped into a third-floor pediatrics ward.

Catfish flopping against lampposts.

Twenty-six head of cattle
wandering main street, three
counties away.

Hay bales on a Norman Roger's
International runway, like they're
planning to travel. Long strips
of linoleum,
                        jiggling slightly

on a lake's surface, covered
                        in young bullfrogs.

Suzie's red enamel, custom panini press
resting at the top of a catalpa tree
on the banks of the Cimarron River.

          She saw it there
          the day she had to get out
          of the house.

SNOW, FLAGSTAFF, ARIZONA

Hand under your sleeping back. Hotel heat.

Locked in, I feel your heart, the loose rattle
of what makes you cough inside your lungs,
encased in blood and skin, moving
with every raw breath.

Out back, snow plows in the parking lot
clearing through the night, *beep beep beep*,
flashing lights, little moraines of ice
against wheel wells.

       You twitch.

Shoulder blades flinching, turning over,
my palm suddenly exposed.

To the left, invisible through walls, and then,
through heavy snow, three steak'n grill places.

     Two highways

in the direction we drove before we stopped.

DEBRIS FLOW, SNOHOMISH COUNTY WASHINGTON

This Oso is my   mountainous love   a mountain's love mountains
of love   muddy   acres of   aching   mountain   dirt current

love.   I am showing you   showering you   giving you my high
ground.   To your river   my raucous mud   my mountainside

drop pouring into you from a sandy crack ripping free from tree line
a streak   my hoarse throat   hollers   stop-gag   slip   *Oso*   I say

Oso Oso.   You say: *I saw   a darkness*   I saw a darkness a darkness
of soil   you say: *Our Oso lips around your full soil*   our homes   soil full

full of soiled me   my limbs   my love   slipped Oso Oso   it's my
forsaken hip! Oso, I shed my hip! Shuddered to you in a snowless

avalanche   took a two-lane rural road   made it my own   you
saw a darkness   Oso a darkness, Oso, my hillside mudslide rain-soaked heavy.

FORCE OF NATURE

Scientists don't necessarily name the places
but speak instead of mid-to-large centres,
are focused on *impact* instead of *precise
dimensions* although I always think of Chicago,
where we met, evolving into us like cities

shaping wingspans of small songbirds,
shorter, blunter limbs for agile flight through
skyscrapers and traffic, the way you and I
balance on a fire escape, gingerly side stepping

my confession of upcoming marriage, watching
raccoons and spiders, each on average three
times larger than their rural counterparts,
our families thinking we're here for business,
or coyotes and foxes adapted to anonymous

garbage foraging under streetlights, nights
far from forests, dens with pups and fish
scents, pavement an econiche, camouflage
to evolutionary biologists observing that while

the size of human thumbs has increased
within a decade of texting, empathy has decreased
with the use of cellphones that alter migration
routes of bees and monarch butterflies as we
Skype to arrange another metropolitan meeting.

OKLAHOMA III

Nuts fallen from splintering pecan trees
in orchards out on the back forty,

little hard-shelled globs of fruity meat, stain
red dirt with pocks of black, composting

and never harvested, your mother dyes
her hair deep brown, almost black,

until her dying day, insisting there's red
Cherokee blood beneath her skin:

walking the flat farm land, slowly
speaking of jaguarundis and soft-shelled

river turtles, of her third husband's family
busting out early, land-run sooners, of caves

where Belle Starr lived and fell, a steady
fascination with things beyond reach.

GO AHEAD AND GIVE YOURSELF OVER TO THE FAULT

of ground, the heaving crack,
the opening-up soil, clay heat
of an earth mouth.

It swallows your bedroom (whole)!

Your bed with you still in it!

Your quilt pillows, duvet headboard.

Your dog and the shag carpet
she rested on, head on paws,
before that unexpected land yawn.

Your Florida dreams (white leather,
frosty-pink marble countertops)
carefully drywalled into reality.

Well done, you, for not fighting it!

Fault lines and other ground
weaknesses are stronger
than any house-buying mistake
you ever made.

I imagine
your new world
in your dirty hole
underneath your
old, deflated house.

The sinkhole is room temperature,
year round, so your dog never stops panting.

Your new walls are not quite brown,
more of a mauvish hue,
the colour of a just-formed scar.
Even you have to laugh
at the impossibility of hospital
corners, a wrinkle-free top sheet.

Never has limestone been of such interest.

You spend all your days now
thinking geologically.

Who knew what was below
all that time, undiscovered
until you fell asleep and were gone?

Earth sounds
all around you.

OUTSIDE, AMERICA

I

Once, slugging Kentucky bourbon from
impossibly thin-walled, clear plastic glasses,
4:13 a.m. in an LA McDonald's parking lot,

our knees touched.
Somewhere along the Drive Thru curve.
Freeways evaporated.

ChevyFordHondaBuick, everything on four
wheels decomposed, a new thick moss.

Satellites clapped
for every metal becoming fog.

II

Then, somewhere in the vicinity
of nine years and thirty-one weeks later,

I am alone, watching out
my living room window.

These two flickers land in the Engelmann
spruce across the road.

If it weren't for the three feet of snow,
they'd have landed on my lawn, the damp soil
much easier to pull up insects from.

Watching me from the same branch,
mated for life.

BROOKLYN FLAT

Ours only for hours, remodelled
grey slate and marble bathroom,
large wine fridge, framed vintage
James Bond poster in the bedroom
that's not ours but staged for first-class
flyers, young men in the financial
sector sighted down the barrel
of Bond's gun, no stove, no oven,
but a microwave and stacks of action-
film DVDs. How when searching
for a knife to cut cilantro and fresh
fruit on the kitchen counter, behind
dusty bags of noodles we find
an expired stash of Warfarin meds
for blood clots and heart arrhythmia,
so we hope no one flatlined here
during some previous short-term rental.
How we talk about that over wine
neither of us knows what temperature
to drink at, but it dulls the hollers
later on, someone insisting there's
an eviction notice pending which ends
up not mattering. Like us arguing
and not dancing because of Hurricane
Sandy flattening so much outer city,
blackening us, and there's sand
and flooding before we leave alone.

Pan	Handle
Great	Plains
Native	America

Back	Forty
Sooners	Boomers
Tornado	Alley

Timmy	McVeigh
Red	Earth
Bible	Buckle

Cattle	Drives
Rose	Rock
Mountain	Lion

Federal	Building
Civilized	Tribes
Oral	Roberts

Okie	Drawl
Done Ready	Done It
Trail	Tears

Grass	Fire
Cock	Fights
Poison	Ivy

DENVER INTERNATIONAL AIRPORT, APRIL

You too might find yourself
in a women's washroom
that doubles as a tornado shelter,
remembering your landing,

looking down on fibreglass,
Blue Mustang, huge horse muscles
taut in an early spring
snowstorm, prairies spread

under raised hooves like a liftoff,
like funnel clouds, you too
might find yourself standing up
to the sound of jets,

dreaming about something bigger
than planes, about being loved
by an astronaut, a man
who has left Earth, crossed

the Atlantic Ocean in six minutes,
witnessed sunset to sunrise
every forty-five minutes,
who talks about riding in a rocket

ship that hums, it's like riding
in a tuning fork struck against metal,
weightlessness, thick as the quiet
inside a hurricane's eye.

PIMA COUNTY, AEROSPACE MAINTENANCE
AND REGENERATION CENTER

On boneyard ground with my one-armed military man,
he's talking Puerto Rican Spanish, laughing, hand off

the wheel of his souped-up silver Mustang, tattooed
hammer of Thor down his chest, twice divorced,

left with the King Charles spaniel, all barky, he wants
to kick it but doesn't, wants to make out in the desert,

to marry someone again, soon, who will change
the bandages on his withered left arm crushed

in a motorcycle accident, a swerve to miss a rabbit,
speeding, coming down from flying, spying on Iraqis,

fighter-plane pilot, we're cruising through the wreckage
fifty years of aerospace science, supersonic Concorde

wing, Boeing turbo engine, props, jet bellies and retired
Air Force Ones shading a shedding coyote, panting.

OKLAHOMA V

Grass fires and ghosts,
something like the cool
of a turned-over pillow
against smoke, mud walls

settling sawdust insulation,
our separation, your mother's
sugar syrup is not twang
but red dirt and dust, not

blood but something close:
coppery poverty, divorce,
heat of cattle ranches,
abandoned banks, new oil.

MOSCOW, IDAHO

It seems always to be about two
meanings, which I don't understand,

sitting across from the small poet
in a local bar that is not local to me

and speaking about the desert, birds,
an autumn bloom of cacti. I know I should

get more from this. When he talks
about activism and, almost crying, confesses

it crushed a desire to fuck, left his marriage
broken. A mountain cougar intercedes

here and there is hiking, loneliness,
wilderness tenting. It all leads to new love

now, metaphors everywhere, how
to write a poem is nature, is sex. I mention

not liking beer. Worry about the paleness
of my thigh, exposed beneath the table.

Was a waitress once like the one he orders
an artisanal brew from. Outside

are all the wheat fields of the Palouse
Range, without me.

A SHORT LIST OF THINGS I SUSPECT AMERICANS DO NOT ASSOCIATE WITH BRITAIN THAT I CONSEQUENTLY LOVE ALL THE MORE

Red kites.
Swifts.
Holts and hay.
Cheddar.
Gorse.
Blewit mushrooms.
Blackberries.
Fireweed.
Scotch pines.
Dartmeet.
Drystone walls.
Slate.
Tits.
Tors.
Wild ponies.
A chalk horse.

IN THE ROGUE BLOOD: AMERICAN NOVEL REDUX, AUGUST 2014

Summer of 1845   but I'm thinking now   right   now
restless(ness) knelt   how forest   fires   how iron   grey
light   of day   ask   engines   failing reckon   a hatful of
eggs   yolk   orange haze on   a full moon   smooth
gravel breached tailings-pond shit, luck don't seem the
word for it, goddamn luck soft

at the flames   he was fixing to   bash   my brains   out
dug   in   the dirt arsenic water   zinc   silt   rock ore
copper belly spasm the brothers   forest fire mining
rupture bore toward the horns wended a dog   growled
in the darkness washes of litter   several mornings   later

mourn forest   scalps freshly salted   smell   hard death
holding close mourn lake creosote in its   steamy
aftermath   a mudded fen sediment jagging   bright
white-wide   yawning, wide-open but a lean man
all things looked to him   sharp-edged and hot to the
touch   in the red light   of the rising

flood   flame   asleep in ashes   *like a man spent on*
a woman gasping wetly whose bones the birds and coyotes
would soon denude of all flesh   later   no one that night
the land lit palely blue with lightning   like a fresh slow
wound where I stand astounded *.the brothers   wild things*
*   of the blood   tense reefs of clouds.*

HONEYMOON ISLAND STATE PARK, FLORIDA

How white the white sand, white
as the egrets, bleached as the sand

and streaked with yellow feathers,
so thin we wonder where wings

are anchored or where big-flying
hearts fit in reedy-white bird bodies

or how the slow, white birds walk
without pain across wide streaks

of snapped-off coral, not yet sand,
our own feet close to bleeding,

walking across sharp shells on this
thin barrier island, split from its other

half in a hurricane before we were
born, before we met and never

honeymooned, before a single pelican
landed close to us, swimming light

in blue salt water against white sand,
with us wondering where our hearts

fit, floating shore-close, watching
white egrets watch dolphins swim

through rips where coral is ground
to sand, under water where once

there was one island, but now
there are two, slender and separate.

NOTES

Poems in this collection have appeared in *The Malahat Review, Lemon Hound, PageBoy Magazine, ElevenEleven: A Journal of Literature and Art* and *CV2.*

ACKNOWLEDGEMENTS

Thank you, you who has walked long distances with me.

Thank you, you who walks short distances with me.

Thank you, you who has read my poetry and offered me your perspective.

Thank you, you who edits my poetry, you who publishes my poetry.

Thank you, you who has travelled America and beyond with me.

Thank you, you who has gotten wet with me at Niagara Falls.

Thank you, you who offers me stories.

Thank you, you who works with me, who helps me work.

Thank you, you who writes with me.

Thank you, you who has been outside with me.

Thank you, you who has stayed inside with me.

Thank you, you who has visited with me.

Thank you, you who has laughed with me, often at me.

Thank you, you who has been my friend and stayed my friend.

Thank you, you who has run trails and tracks with me.

Thank you, you who has cared for me.

Thank you, you who meets me.

Thank you, you who hasn't given up on me.

Thank you, you who is kinder than me and inspires me.

Thank you, you who has been patient.

Thank you, you who has taught me and is still teaching me.

Thank you, you who I know has suffered such loss.

Thank you, you who lives with me.

Thank you, you the place I live.

Thank you, you the land I love.

Thank you, you the land I love on.

Thank you, you.

Thank you.

ABOUT THE AUTHOR

Sarah de Leeuw is an award-winning Canadian writer and researcher. Her books include *Unmarked: Landscapes Along Highway 16* (NeWest Press, 2004), *Front Lines: Portraits of Caregivers in Northern British Columbia* (Creekstone Press, 2011), *Geographies of a Lover* (NeWest Press, 2012), *Skeena* (Caitlin Press, 2015) and *Where it Hurts* (NeWest Press, 2017). *Geographies of a Lover* won the Dorothy Livesay BC Book Prize and *Where it Hurts* was a finalist for the Governor General's Literary Award for non-fiction and a finalist for the Roderick Haig-Brown Regional BC Book Prize. Her essays have won two CBC literary awards and a Western Magazine Gold Award. She divides her time between Prince George and Kelowna, BC.

PHOTO CREDIT: BRIAR CRAIG